SALVAGE

SALVAGE

• poems •

Thomas Aslin

Thomas Aslin (signature)

LOST HORSE PRESS
Sandpoint, Idaho

ACKNOWLEDGMENTS

Some of these poems have appeared in the following publications:

Hubbub: "The Quilt Maker"
One: "A Portrait in White"

My thanks to my late parents, Florence and Fred Aslin; to the Madrona Writers; to Tom Mitchell; to Al Maginnes for his friendship and inspiration; to Jordan Hartt for his close reading of the poems; to Gary Thompson for his astute comments and suggestions; and to Joseph Stroud whose suggestions worked their way into these poems in more ways than I know.

Cover Art: Z.Z. Wei, *Palouse Shadows.* This and other fine paintings by Seattle artist Z.Z. Wei can be viewed online at www.zzweiart.com.

Author Photo: Mary Hoisington.

Book & Cover Design: Christine Holbert.

FIRST EDITION

This and other fine LOST HORSE PRESS titles may be viewed online at www.losthorsepress.org.

LIBRARY OF CONGRESS CATALOGING-IN-PUBLICATION DATA
Names: Aslin, Thomas, 1963 - author.
Title: Salvage : poems / Thomas Aslin.
Description: First edition. | Sandpoint, Idaho : Lost Horse Press, 2016.
Identifiers: LCCN 2016028283 | ISBN 9780996858441 (trade paper : alk. paper)
Classification: LCC PS3601.S598 A6 2016 | DDC 811/.6—dc23
LC record available at https://lccn.loc.gov/2016028283

for Richard Hugo

HOW I NEVER KNEW THE REASON

(a cento)
for Richard Hugo

All these years I never told a soul about
what happened to you there,
the phone call from the hospital.
How I never knew the reason.

Beneath the north star long enough
I fight the sudden cold diminished light.
Unafraid of roses, I still believe
you and I can love there
and stand there, each suddenly alone.

Daylight has a way of seeping in.
And you come back here
for the first time.

Downriver behind us
it is much the same . . .
not much better . . .

When the mill shuts down
not even birds can raise the dust.

When Italians
move away, the air hangs silent as a pear.

TABLE OF CONTENTS

FINDING MY UNCLE AT DONNA'S CAFE

I find him there chewing on a toothpick
and chatting with friends before rising
from the table, before tossing a quarter
in a bowl for a cigarette. Back at the house
he touches the scar over his brow,
says an English doctor saved his life,
then rolls up his pant leg to reveal
a scar like a small, white squid.
He says it was a dum-dum bullet broke his tibia.
"Can you believe it?
I was shot by a twelve year old."

As evening settles in,
Brutus, their old, gray tom,
paces the kitchen floor, mewing.
My aunt lets him out, checks his food,
his water, his litter. Above the valley floor
the moon a thin, bone ladle.
After dinner, a gloss of stars smeared
across the heavens, I call for him.
Later he lies at the foot of my bed.
On the wall above the chest of drawers, a seascape:
a shell-like scroll of waves striping the shore.

As much as anything
it is the laughter and the welcome light
and the thin thread of a story that find
their way to a room. Afraid of the dark
when I was small, I'd pry my bedroom door
ajar so I could hear my parents, my uncle and my aunt.
Even from my room I knew my uncle
draped his forearms over the back of a kitchen chair,

that he rode the chair as if astride
a piebald pony, cutting a sickly heifer from the herd.
Laughing, the men smoked, they sipped their beer.
The women spoke of white sales and children.

THE QUILT MAKER

for Mary Hoisington

Not to stitch something
from the time she has is an idleness
that doesn't rest easy with her.

And knowing
what she'd rather not know
hasn't made the task any easier.

So the day came when she
purchased a building site
above the lake she has loved
since she was a child.

A house was made to order
on a slope above the deepest water.

Even the dimmed light
that first winter, the unease of it
having entered the framed rooms,
was a vision worth holding.

So enter here: a crisp, snow bound
winter scene. A house. A lake.
A sable hillside across the water.
Snow finds its way here each year.
From the heavens it comes,
from the close sky.

Not to fashion what she can
from the time that is left
invites a restlessness.

When she cannot sleep
the woman of the house takes
remnants from the sky, the snow,
the hillside, the water, and the stars,
from the runic scheme of frost on the windows
and her own feral dream to fashion a quilt.
Take notice of the color along the fence line,
along the bank of snow.
This is the quilt maker's field.

The woman in the house
on the lake has been at work.

A BUS DRIVER'S JOURNAL

First thing in the morning
the wind and a near opalescence
feather across the lake.
Though within hours a young woman
gives herself a hot-shot in the rear of the bus.
There are days, despite what is surely
the divinest light, when there's
no helping us.

•

I want to say this kind of thing isn't an everyday occurrence
until the heavy man leaning against the stanchion
falls to the floor. It takes two men to wrestle
a dead man through a door.

•

Half way into the novel I've been reading,
an old man fills a cigarette paper with tobacco,
licks the paper and lights it,
the kitchen match struck across the teeth of his fly.
Taking a deep draw of air and smoke,
he slumps face first in the oatmeal set before him.
The waitress says he always has a cigarette first thing
in the morning, his oatmeal getting cold.

•

This evening my clothes smell like diesel.
The floor of the bus like piss.
Only two things can make me forget my sore back,
my stiff, swollen knee: a hot bath
and a slow, sentient fuck.

•

My father says a man working for wages
will never get rich. Never.
The room settles into silence.
I'm living proof of that I say.
Just more fish bait, I whisper under my breath.

•

Floyd, a sweet, old man, boards my bus
at the reservoir, says his wife died last month.
His face collapses when he speaks.
He's someone you'd want to hold, if you were able,
like your mother held you when you were a baby
flush with a fever.

•

Divorced last October, I've been told of late
to fuck myself more ways than I care to remember,
and then told with uncommon erudition
to have at my mother too.
A friend says, so what did you say or do
to piss these people off ?
A field supervisor, who can't distinguish
his own face from his ass
in rain or snow with either hand, says,
"You're the one who has a problem."

•

Yesterday a full moon like few I've seen
shone light like chrome along a narrow, paved road.
So many ugly or soiled things, then this . . .

•

Months storm by and Floyd boards my bus on Roosevelt,
says he's fallen in love.
I say love is a good thing, Floyd, a damn fine thing.
I think I was nearly as happy for him as he was.

•

My mother calls me when she calls me
from within my dreams only,
and there is no getting around the void one feels.
While driving at night or resting a bit
at the end of the line, you know those hard-drinking men
who ride the bus ride the bus mostly for the heat.

•

What follows is nothing if not sad. The day comes
when Floyd tells me he's been taken to the cleaners.
Those aren't his words. His words are touched
with the love he feels for the woman.
And when he speaks he looks nothing if not a little lost.
No surprise there.
My father would've said he's been fleeced.
That's about as pure as metaphor gets
and no less a tragedy.
I tell Floyd there's no shame in falling in love,
no shame whatsoever.

•

No matter how all this turns out,
and I have my suspicions,
there are mornings with the wind flagging
when a man hopes to absolve himself and others
for the harm we've done, the harm we do.

Twice I asked for directions before turning at the county dump: a
hundred gulls hawking their rusty screes over hillocks of diapers
and sour milk, sodden news-print and orange rinds. Having made
a U-turn I found Ocean View high above the strait, found his name
scrawled in trochees on a card wired to a pike stuck firmly in the
ground. The black stone edifice, gravestone and bench, not yet in
place, so the fragment of poetry etched in polished rock is not in
place, nor the photograph by the renowned photographer that now
unites husband and wife above ground. Near the grave two men
raised a concrete slab with a pry bar. I offered, "So who's moving?"
I was told a woman died the previous week and just then they were
preparing her vault. A bit tired and distracted, I turned to face the
water, to watch a raven bathe in a pool of fresh rain. This fall with
his grave in place, what I found unnerving when I arrived was not
the grave, despite its size, but the small gathering of young men and
women near it. Three garlands of flowers and four potted plants
lying near their feet. The young people dressed as if on their way to
dinner before their homecoming dance and by some mistake have
stopped here. On this afternoon I keep my thoughts to myself, stay
only long enough to mull over the words on the grave, to conjure
a man I met once over coffee and cigarettes, a man known for how
closely he listened, for the pains he took to hear what was said. A
friend once revealed that Ray was always trolling for material, as
this was his habit, though when he spoke, he spoke so softly you had
to lean as close as he had to catch his words. And when he smiled,
after all the years of smoking and drinking, you couldn't help but
see his teeth were the color of old ivory or in lesser light cold rain.
On this visit what I hear are the gulls circling the dump. And I see
the strait where it has always been. Rumor is his widow wore a
path around his plot before his gravestone was ever set in place.

And upon hearing as much, you know it must be true. On my drive this morning the thin band of light along the canal turned from ochre to residual gold leaf. And a dozen blue herons stood nearly motionless on a sandbar near the reservation. I've heard it is an omen to see so many in one place. Must be a kind of luck, I whispered, to have come this far to visit the dead.

RESIDUE

First a smattering of rain plies the leaves
before sheets of lightning flare
in the distance: what your father called
heat lightning. The weather is temperate,
even listless, before the maples along the walk
are dressed down in the time it takes
to draw a breath. With the storm
comes a more pronounced branching of light,
a rumbling of Thor's kettle drum.
As you touch finger to thumb, you count
in a voice unlike any you remember.
A lover said once lightning does not strike
from the sky but rises as charged ions
to meet other charged particles in the ether.
Just now thunder and lightning arrive
as one, or so you hear it.
A sharp report, a tree split in half.
Without discernible shadow
a hallelujah of white, fulminating light.
The screened-in porch of the century old house
shakes. How were you to understand
the absence of shadow without ever having seen
this annealing light? After several minutes
a light comes on in the house across the street.
With morning there's a residue of shadow
on the lawn. On the walk near the maples
all that's left of the rain.

BIRTHDAY POEM

for Madeline DeFrees

Bordering your house a chain-link fence
draped in the tendrils of clematis montana.
I see you rise from your chair
near a small table stacked with books
and papers to peer out a south window
to the fence. Taking another sip of coffee
you open the screen door, then step
gingerly down several narrow steps
to approach the creamy blooms.
You are drawn, I believe, to the undercurrents
of color, to a scent of vanilla with a touch of honey.

Blossoms this beautiful and woven this close
have an obvious fragility. You reach for a blossom,
then touching it draw it near.

Not long ago while I was visiting,
I turned to hear you say
there were too many blossoms this year
and their bouquet was cloying and too sweet.

I cannot give you what I wish—
a near surfeit of time and beauty,
but I was certain when I left that day
that you'd awake the next morning,
have a cup of rich, dark roast, then peer
from your bay window, holding in your gaze
a vision unlike any
you might have seen.
And I envision what I believe you saw that day—

a fence overburdened with its freight of beauty.
And no matter where I find myself
in the seasons ahead, whenever I see
delicate blossoms shouldering such
fearsome beauty, I am certain to think of you.

AT THE POET'S READING

after Stanley Plumly

It's his voice gives him away.
There is a catch in his breath.
So when he finishes reading
the poem he wrote on Keats
and John Constable and the clouds
Constable painted on Hampstead Heath,
he remarks how poems surprise you
sometimes. Keats's death is stirring up
emotion, as is the beauty of Constable's
inimitable clouds, as is his own friable breath,
so light, heavy of heart.
He speaks of Hampstead and these men
who lived a short distance from each other
and yet never met. He says Keats
should never have left the heath.
What remains when he's finished reading
his poem is his memory of a poet walking
on a narrow, cobbled path that leads
to the Englishman's grave. Vertigo
overcomes him. So he steps awkwardly
from the wavering path, then coughs
so hard and long he is afraid to bring
the cloud-white handkerchief to his mouth.
In a corner, near the cornice of the wall
nearest the grave he finds the name he is
looking for. In the muted grass a tabby cat
lies just behind the damp side of the stone.

PARIS WITH RAIN

for Michael and Toni Hanner

Two friends arrive in Paris today.
And though I am mostly at a loss
these days, were I there I would walk
with them to a modest cafe
on the avenue Suffren, order
the canard confit: a tasty waterfowl
cooked on a low, steady heat
in its own lovely fat.
My mother refused to prepare the ducks
my father brought home. She did not like
their gamey taste. My father knew this.
In his bones he knew this or should have.

I hear rain is stippling the avenues
of the city this week. Showers
interrupted only by the briefest reveal
of sun, thin emanations of azure sky
obliquely visible. As good a time
as any to climb the narrow steps
of the south tower of Notre Dame,
to gaze upon the Seine, to catch
a peripheral view of a winged beast
spewing water to the square below.
Charlemagne vigilant as ever
on his stone horse. A wet, cold day
makes the duck confit taste all the better
in a city known for light
and for grievous shadow.

WIND AND THE ROSES

Such a winter we've had.
If the weather is willing,
I plan to spread coffee grounds
in a mulch for the roses.
So cheer up, my hothouse beauties.

There's a peculiar, musky scent
before a long awaited rain.
Water, or rather the lack of it,
wears at our resolve till finally
a surfeit of rain and wind arrive.
Mostly our winter came late this year,
a month into the spring.

I hoped to put a few uneasy dreams
to rest this evening. Whatever beliefs
I held once wore off years ago,
though what I hear in the trees
through the window is speech
of a kind, a glossolalia of a sort.
My mother was a true believer
and as such what she fashioned
with her hands (dresses of her own
design and slip covers with piping
for our couch and wing-backed chair)
was stitched with a tensile strength,
a kind of intricate grace. My late teacher,
a poet, when speaking of the sacred
referenced wind and only wind, never God.
So perhaps the sound the wind and leaves foment
is enough after all. For when I slip to my knees
and ask for a touch of mercy,
it is wind and only the wind I hear
stirring among the leaves.

QUESTIONS AND ANSWERS

Why did you do it?

Because I knew no other way.
Because I could not be anyone other than who I was.

Why did you leave then?

Because the moon left most of its feathers on the water in the bay.
Because my voice like my father's
    when angry raises the hackles on my neck.

Why did you not seek out the divine?

Because I have no belief in an absolute.
Because any abstraction is difficult to believe or define.

Why did you turn from the locked gate toward the wind off the bay?

Because the wind touches most everything.
Because a latch fits so cleanly into a hasp.

What troubled you the most?

Because I did not know how to love her,
    she whispered another's name.
Because I was hurt I made something hurtful from what was said.

What lingers with you on the longest nights?

Because I broke my hand on the wall, the wall is often with me.
Because of the wall on the coldest, wettest evenings
    I know where I've been.

AND THE DAYS ARE NOT FULL ENOUGH

(a cento)

Every living thing in bloom there.
Out of the light evolved the moving blooms.
Either to other,
The blossoms sang
And faded through the brightening air
To feed their mother-root when they have blown.
What you are, root and all, and all in all
When yellow leaves, or none, or few, do hang.
The leaves believe
The lively, lovely air.
I agree with the leaves.

No one except those I knew
Of night and light and the half-light—
And the nights are not full enough.
Through the roaring cars, the hum of tires, the closing of doors
Coming from far off . . . and the sweet clear
That comes and goes in silences of its own.
At midnight when the house falls quiet,
The wind moves slowly in the branches.
I once more smell the dew and rain.

IF NOT FOR A STONE

There was a time when the citizenry
of New Orleans buried their dead
in cypress coffins. Cypress, however,
is so buoyant that after a hard rain
the coffins were apt to rise
from out of the ground and float off.
So then the city fathers built walls
around the cemeteries to keep their dead close
and to keep passersby from seeing in.
This, however, was a temporary fix at best,
so gravediggers began cutting holes
in each coffin lid and burying their dead
with heavy stones over their hearts.
As such the dead were not so different
from the rest of us, whose hearts grow
heavy from time to time, even as we take our rest.

TRIXI'S "ANTLER" BAR BLUES

for Gary Thompson, Tom Crawford, and Paul Zarzyski

Paul rolls up in his '63 Olds from Great Falls.
Gary and Tom spend the morning clearing deadfalls.
Driving from Missoula, I answer a siren's baleful call.

The four of us meet early one evening at Trixi's "Antler" Bar.
Four men sit down for a drink at Trixi's roadside bar.
Through the window the rosy leavings of the morning star.

Laughter limns the room as our waitress makes her rounds.
Thompson reels off a story and buys another round.
Nothing keeps us from laying our troubles down.

Paul says he was sorry to hear Walt Pavlich passed on.
I say, what with fathers and all, there's a lot of that going on.
As we live and breathe, we learn to live on our own.

Four men hoist a drink under a white tail's head and antlers.
The four of us evoke Hugo and Carver in a bar filled with antlers:
the air thick with what passes for ghosts in a smoky bar.

Just now the waitress plays the Wurlitzer and dishes up a song.
On a downbeat Johnny Cash tears into that Folsom Prison song.
When he shoots a man in Reno *just to watch him die,* we sing along.

AMERICAN SENTENCES

The rain on the street speaks
most insistently when a semi passes.

The whinny of the policeman's horse
is heard in the young girl's laughter.

On paving just behind the Mustang
and ticking engine, a road apple steams.

Shrink-wrapped with the sweetbreads
and liver is the tongue.

What more is there to say of the moon
and the river but what has been said?

Yesterday the poet spoke movingly
of the sweetbreads of the soul.

On Mondays the Barlow Farm Labor Tavern
serves dollar pitchers of beer.

Not all birds speak at once. This morning
only the mourning doves under the eaves.

The door in the floor of the dream
allows me to stay afloat in the river.

The moon on the water is the rumor
of the shadow of the moon.

AFTER PRAXILLA OF SICYON

Loveliest of what I leave behind
is for others to say. Not much,
I suspect. A palimpsest, perhaps,
of a father's diurnal rage,
a glimpse into the hospital room
where my mother lay dying.
And in her room a small gift:
tiny boats made of walnut shells
riding the thin edge of a light breeze
just this side of a window that looks
out onto wheat fields and orchards
simmering in the late afternoon light.

PALOUSE

From a distance a patchwork of fields.
On the butte blue-eyed grass, a gully wash,
variegated light in the fescue. Wildflowers
and prairie stars where I stand. Cattle
below look small, not the behemoths grandfather raised.
Difficult to compare these with cattle my father's feed

fattened. After thirty years my father the last feed
dealer in the valley. South of town the fields
a burnished mustard. Each rise
of land under the sun or sere moon awash
in wheat and oats limned with light: the cattle
working their cuds, the hay and steer ration from the flour

mills in Colfax and Spangle. Years ago flour
mills built along the Spokane River fed
a local need for bread. If not for this, for the cattle,
the hay bales and sacked grain, these fields
would seem merely ornamental, even in the clear wash
of a pocked moon or wheel of sun rising.

I love a yeasty moon rising,
run up the sky like a flag. No harrier or flower
more grave or more beautiful in such an ethereal wash.
And nothing feeds
an eye as a red-tailed hawk on a post. I miss the fields
in the morning and evening, the cattle

lowing. My grandfather's last cattle
ranch laid out on a table of land risen
high above the Snake: pasture and hay fields,
wild roses and sprigs of purple flower.
Outbuildings and house where my uncle and aunt fed
a family with the beef they raised. A wash

of sturgeon and steelhead in a river reconciles a wash
of northern light with flyways for geese, hay fields for cattle.
Nothing much more than a magpie is needed to feed
such a dream. This and the certainty of a moonrise,
stars spread like wildflowers,
vetch inching up the bluffs to the fields.

Balsam root and thistle. Cattle left to graze. A sunrise
over prairie smoke and lupine, clover in flower,
a light wind washing across the fields.

WHITE LILAC

A cloud-like, snow-white lilac leans into the fencing.
With the air a bit torpid last evening,
what to make of a warbler's febrile call this morning?

There is little doubt a squall is making its approach.
Weathered palings shore up the pale bush and panicles:
the bowed remains of a fence is home for a lovely contagion.

Difficult to assess wind without walking or standing
in it. After a summer storm such as this, one is left
with a blue, unsullied expanse of sky this morning.

The fields my grandfather plowed and seeded are the fields
I find at the base of the butte. I look to old photographs.
Where the garden was, gooseberry and lilac flourish.

I wish my grandfather were here. I'd drive us to the VFW
for an early dinner, an evening of stud poker, an ice-cold beer.
My wish for the untenable is not unusual this morning.

Near the barn a fresh wind stirs where the scent of lilac lingers.
A Cooper's hawk alights on telephone wire along the road,
close to where lilacs sprawl along the fence,
close to where a warbler and meadowlark perch this morning.

WINTER SOLSTICE

In memory, Jack Collier (b. 1914 - d. 1942)

There's no mystery in this: with winter in the air
entire sections of wheat, oats, and sorghum lie dormant.
The acres etched crudely with harrows are a dun color
or after a squall a thick gumbo. Though what you
would have seen that day north of the hen house
is a woman running across hardpan fronting the barn.
And this is no season to gloss over what was to follow:
the undulant fever, an aging father blaming himself
for letting the bacteria take hold. At dawn the man
herds his steers into a corral and shoots every
damn one. Pours diesel over each animal,
then touches off a guttering fire. Even as
an underbelly of cloud settles in beneath the sun,
it's the three year old finds his father hanging in the barn.

LOOKING THROUGH PHOTOGRAPHS
AT HER SISTER'S HOUSE

for Sherry Freshwater

With family photographs strewn
across the table, I ask my cousin,
Sherry, about the mixed-breed terrier
I was told could talk. She says, "Yes,
that was Brownie," then plucks
a black and white image from the pile,
points to a small dog with a dark mask
sitting on the front stoop and says,
"Yes, he could talk." So I ask,
what would he say? She says
though he understood more than
a hundred words, he said two things.
She says, "He said *ma ma,*" pausing
as he might have between each laving
syllable. Then straining as he might have
for the tone and reach of a small dog's
feral range, she says, "Out." And with this,
reflecting back from some distance
she is at once removed, in both body and soul,
to our grandmother's house on Sprague Avenue.
Then with tears in her eyes, and her throat
tightening, she says, "It was boys who killed him.
Shot him with a BB gun."

She was seven. Her mixed-breed dog
dragged himself home. She says,
"I could have killed them."
Then she says, with a voice touched

with forgiveness, what she has
always wanted to believe: "They were
just boys, just boys being boys."

DRIFTING TOWARD SLEEP
IN HEDGEROW, NORMANDY 1944

His company crabbed
along the beach in a lateral rain.
Cleared the battery,
the machine gun nest.
Near Saint Lo another company dogface
clipped the sniper in the steeple.
Three days of slogging in mud
brings him here to this field.

From Tilly-sur-Seulles
another shelling.
Salt on his skin, on the uniform.
So many have fallen
in this hedgerow of sweet chestnut
and beech, bullfinches and blackcaps,
yellowhammer bunting.

As he drifts toward sleep . . .

Vivian cores the lemon,
squeezes juice on her hands.

An astringent he recalls her saying.

A tart sweetness, he says
in a reedy voice
as thin as the leaf he fingers,
this smell of toasted almonds
and lemon . . .

He recalls the cherry blossoms
he walked to before leaving . . .
the last clean faces he saw
before shipping out.

With first light this morning,
a whiff of cordite . . .
and in the distance not light so much as
encaustic smeared on a thin, dark strip of canvas,
the stain of burnt sienna to the east.

LATE HARVEST

I miss the sheaths of wheat
on the Lincoln penny,
miss the wind leveling off
across the burnished grain behind the barn.
With all the hydroelectric work
and concrete pours on the Snake
the few who lived on its banks
moved off the river, moved their dead.

And it was the Herefords on the ranch
above Central Ferry and on the farm
near Steptoe that put my grandfather
in the driver's seat of a new Imperial
every two years, that prompted him
to drive to Denver and to San Francisco
and the Cow Palace with grandmother
for auctions and shows.

In this day of specialization
my cousin custom cuts wheat,
spends hours in the lurid sun,
then dry-tills the ground.
This and nothing else is what
he does for work these days.

Behind my hotel this morning
the moon is slightly out-of-round.
Where I sleep nestled up against
the North Sea, I am comfortable enough.

One hears a storm is cleansing,
is a blessing, though last night

after a hard, ravening rain,
a small ground fire smoldered
in an early dream, an electrical burn
in another.

Though nothing prepared me
for the texture or colors
in van Gogh's *Four Sunflowers.*

Finding a bench to sit on in the gallery,
I stared at the painting for an hour.
Even with the stalks cut,
with the crowns of seeds lying about,
the flowers retain a touch of star-fire,
draw me inexorably
to the southern verge of the garden
my grandfather kept on his farm.

A PORTRAIT IN WHITE

Because I could not write
I drew grocery lists for my mother,
drew a tape dispenser that resembles
a Henry Moore elephant, drew
a toothbrush and a scrolled tube of paste,
a comb baring misshapen teeth.
Along the margins Mother inscribed
the name of each. Later when I could
write but could not spell,
she continued to print the names
of each object I drew.
For all I knew these early efforts
showed little, if any artistic promise
though my mother thought otherwise.
My talent, as I saw it, was in knowing
what to leave out. Upon sketching
our house but unsure how to draft or shade
a flagstone path, I covered each stone,
as God might, with billows of snow.
When furnishing the bedrooms in the house,
I covered my sleeping figures with sheets
drawn to their chins. Only their heads
or an errant hand exposed. The Springer
Spaniel was easy in comparison.
She slept in the patio next to the garage,
so from my point of view was invisible.
Though from where I sit today the figures
in my stark rooms seem etherized or worse.
And since my parents are deceased
and my brothers and I seldom speak,
my primitive sketches were prescient.
Given pencil and paper a small child
drew a future he never would have imagined.

HORSE PISS

My mother says horse piss in an empty kitchen.

In my father's mother's house near town, the TV squalls.

A clarion voice fills the family room with evangelical weather,

a kind of water. There is a bit of wind beyond the bay window

and the sill. Leaves are moving. The larger pot is stirring.

My mother's mother is dying, though my mother does not know this.

She has her hands full with laundry soap and bleach and kerosene

and her own prognosis. She knows of wind in the locust leaves.

She sees the trees bucking in the neighbor's yard. At the feed store

my father horses a hundred-weight bag of pea pellets into a Pontiac wagon.

The smell of feed never leaves the store and mill, is there in the morning,

much of it sweet, or nearly so. At home our soiled laundry lies in a wicker

hamper. Another work shirt pressed, the steam iron hisses and spits.

The John Deere tractor on the Central Ferry ranch hisses if overheated.

Beside himself, my grandfather helps my grandmother, Maude, to the car,

drives her to Colfax: the wind following them nearly out of breath.

A man's manicured hand assigns *consumptive heart failure* to her chart.

In the paddock the brindle mare buries her nose in the rolled oats.

A Kenworth pulling a trailer of hay bales from the valley floor,

gears down then gears down again. The mare sidles up

to the water trough. My mother folds her fresh laundry—

bed sheets, T-shirts and briefs, towels and wash cloths.

ORANGE

Upon waking this morning
I thought of one singular afternoon.
Mother and I were alone in the house
when she took me aside to instruct me
in the delicate art of administering her shots.
It might come to this, she said.
I recalled also, a Thursday evening class
in which a young poet rhymed phalange
with orange. Our teacher, a beloved man,
feigned scorn. My rhyme this morning,
what those who write poetry call a slant-
or half-rhyme, must have simmered
within me for years, before I dredged it up
like that odd stone that rests on my desk,
a rock with distinct striations that I plucked
from the silt of the river where my father fished.
My mother asked me, with a syringe in one hand
and a ripening orange in the other,
if I might learn to administer *her* shots.
You hear that off rhyme, don't you—syringe
with orange? Not so different from the young poet's
phalange and orange, though I was not to track
my mother's finger or metacarpal bones
but the veins in the crook of her arm,
as she tied off her arm at the elbow, bringing
a single vein to the surface so I might see
where to slide the needle, the thin gauge needle
into her arm. I think I broke off all discussion
then and there. I didn't trust myself, was afraid
I'd miss the vein. We didn't get past the orange
and syringe that day. I could go on, say more
about the young poet in class or about our late teacher.

I could say more about my mother and my having
rhymed syringe with orange, but I want to say
how fearful I became sitting near my mother,
holding the orange and syringe, one in each hand.
I must have handed that orange and narrow gauge
needle to her. I must have said something
before rising from the chair,
before walking into the other room.

A MOTHER'S HAND

Light shoulders the ineffable,
an untenable hold on shadow.
When I awaken to the susurrous
wheeze of wind sifting through
the window screen, whatever I
question has a desultory feel.
So when I turn and lean close
to you, my strain of grief
is a stone of disbelief—
your hand in mine
a blue-veined leaf.

BECAUSE MY MOTHER WAS BEAUTIFUL

a man named Daly
eloped with her, this young ingenue,
when she was seventeen.
Within days their vows were annulled.
Her brother tells me this.
I suspect too much Canadian whiskey,
a tempest of rough-hewn epithets,
a closed fist, a young bride
sprawled on the kitchen floor.

And it was my father's brother, Armand,
who introduced my father and mother
near the tennis courts at Mission Park.
And because my father was taken with
her hazel eyes, her slim ankles,
her patrician hands, he pursued her.

When later she posed for the photograph
my father carried overseas, she wore
a crushed velvet hat and camelhair coat,
pencil lines drawn on each calf to simulate
nylon stockings. She was, as was said then,
comely. Even in her thirties, she turned heads.

When my mother died,
her sister-in-law, Ethel,
dressed my mother in an ivory
silk blouse and herringbone skirt,
washed and combed her hair,
put lipstick to her lips, a touch of rouge
to her cheeks. Upon arriving
at the funeral home early in the evening,

I caught a glimpse of the young woman
my father lived with before the war.
And by standing near her,
as if in still water,
I gazed at her without shame
for as long as I wished.

A VIEW OF THE MISSION RANGE
FROM ST. IGNATIUS

The nurse
says, "How are you?
Can you make a fist, dear?"
In the small room, she probes your skin.
She hopes

tying
off your right arm
at the elbow will yield
a vein, though works to find even
one. You

lie there
several hours.
The IV fluid drips.
Time, a thistle-like scourge, wears on
you, pulse

by pulse.
Each arm prodded
yields a colorful bruise.
Conjure a *Rand-McNally Map*
of States.

Scarlet
for interstates,
county roads royal blue.
A white cross on the shoulder marks
a death.

No one
strains to obscure
what took place here. A cross
does little to lighten the loss.
Due west

from near
the Mission Range
five crosses on the bridge
flaunt a cautionary bouquet.
Mother,

how long
has it been since
we have spoken? Forty
winters I'd guess. Father said once,
not to

worry,
there is no end.
He was nearing ninety
and rushing toward his own death.
How I

wish to
believe him, though
you would say I remain
as doubtful as the apostle,
Thomas.

I want
none of it. And
though I want to believe,

seems you were prescient. Nearing
the church

I pull
to the shoulder,
leave the warm car: the peaks
north of the mission scoured with ice,
with wind.

A BRIEF SKETCH

In the backyard you empty
your pant cuffs, spiking
the flower bed with red wheat
and rolled oats, alfalfa
and cracked corn.

If I were to sketch you
I'd begin here in this light
and hone in on your eyes,
your swarthy face, your hair
with that dark, wet obsidian shine.
Then I'd render your strong, broad hands.
And having finished this, I'd disassemble
the scene, sketch the Sacred Heart of Jesus
blazing on the calendar on the wall,
the Sunbeam toaster on the table,
your right fist clenched against
the kitchen wall: a sad coterie
of Mother's family
sitting in the front room,
speaking ever so softly.

ANOTHER LOVE POEM

In a cafe I frequent
Peggy Lee sings *Goody, Goody.*
Her voice coming from the speaker
mounted near the ceiling.
She stretches notes with a voice
filled with light and ether,
not the smoky, slightly abraded voice
of later years. Just now she warms up
to *Imagination,* although with both
the dishwasher and freezer running
I can't be sure how far she has waded
into the song. She's become part
of a conversation I can't quite follow.
At the table behind me three older women
speak. I hear one say, "He must have had
seizures." Peggy shifts down a key.
Now she's in love or so burns the song
she is singing. But then all good songs
are torch songs, just as all good poems
are love poems of a kind. In her
honey-blonde youth Peggy must have
wrenched more than a few hearts.
A few years ago a woman I was seeing
said all men are dogs. I resisted saying
what I thought. As of late I've been listening
to the words of a lovely woman I met not long ago.
And when she reads this, I know she'll have
something to say. She may even shake her head
and exclaim, "Oh, Jesus, not another love poem."
And all I will say is what I have wanted to say all along,
"If I said I was sorry I wouldn't mean it."

THE POET IS SURPRISED BY THE
APPEARANCE OF A NAKED ADMIRER

for Julie

In a cozy room overlooking a small, formal garden,
I am overwhelmed by the sheer size of the plane tree
just beyond the mullioned windows. It reaches
with its freshest leaves to the glass panes.
I'm sitting at a weathered desk, stray marks imbedded
in the surface. Several hammer marks visible:
annular moons in wood stained an earthen brown.
This early the shadows outside the window seem
to broaden and lengthen, though I know at this time
of day this cannot be true. After all, it is only because
dawn is near that I see them at all. There's a cat
on the fence. No, not there but to your left.
And a dog's plaintive call is audible. Hearing
a distant siren I understand his response.
Again I have had a restless night. Not so unusual
these days, though I am pleased I am working on
poems in the home of a lovely woman I've come
to know. She writes, when she writes, of water.
Her writing reflecting just how much water there is
in our lives, in our cells. So as not to frighten me
she allows me to hear her enter the room.
As she draws near, she touches me about the shoulder
and neck. She is warm from her bed. In this light
I don't see the fresh scar she wears. I've come here
as surprised as any. I don't share my darkest thoughts
with her, though I suspect she knows of them.
And she knows only the harshest of events
brought me here. Early this morning when I awoke
and saw her sleeping, I wanted to paint her.

There is much to reveal of her. Like the English painter
I have studied, I'd use an oatmeal shade, umber and
earthen hues, creams and yellows, dark forest green.
And if she were to awake while I was working,
I would say not to worry, my dear, I will need
years of careful, considered study to get this right

HEART OF THE COLEUS

for J.T.
In memoriam, S.W.

After the sheet is pulled over
the inert body
and the door is closed softly
and a cloud slides between the sun and
the plate glass window, the heart within
the leaf of the coleus darkens a bit.

•

Once during a hard winter
ice formed on both sides of my window.
The space heater warming nothing
but the center of the room.
Its coils as bright as the coals
in the furnace of my childhood home.
What is left to forgive
when all one remembers of her
besides a prolonged absence
is her inimitable smell and voice?

•

Across the street from Garden City News
the Hmong sell beautiful peaches and plums.
Leeks and onions, spinach and chard.
An old man with red hair brandishes
a Bible like a handgun. He says,
"Turn to John 23 or risk losing your soul.
Read Paul's letter to the Ephesians."
He stops for a moment, pulls at his crotch,

then rails some more. The heart
within the heart of the coleus
exceeds its borders.
Despite all, there is great beauty here.

•

Last winter a friend said, "I am swimming
in my own Cold Duck soup." Then with the wind
storming over his shoulder he took a swig
from the bottle he held in his hand saying,
"This, this is my personal anti-freeze."

•

My uncle repaired his favorite boots
with a glue gun, trapped cougars in a trap
he'd made. His daughter says his heart
seized-up like a water pump. He died
mid-sentence, rose up off the bed
as if on tenterhooks, as if raised part way to heaven.
The floor nurse in the room asked her
if she wouldn't please finish her father's story.

•

Stopping at the White Horse Tavern
I knew little of the poet who drank himself
to death. The emergency room physician finished him
with morphine. The coroner said he died from an insult
to the brain. Imagine him lying there, clothes stripped
from his body, his vital signs taken and filed.
His watch and wallet and several shillings slipped
into the gaping mouth of a Manila envelope.
His clothes and his skin harboring the pungent smell
of cigarette smoke and sweat.
An almost sweet smell. Almost.

•

In Missoula last fall Julie and I
ordered drams of Scotch from Isley,
from the Highlands, from the Outer Hebrides.
My whisky smelled like the scorched carpet
and bedding we found in the burned out cabin
near Mount Index where a man lay lifeless a year ago.
I didn't dream this. Neither did she.
A dream this harsh is a truth
one would hope to awaken from.
On occasion she fears she'll lose me.

•

By any measure this has been a difficult year.
Friends going to sleep and not waking.
Or sleeping then waking to say a word
or two before dying.
I am not ashamed to say I speak to the dead.
Though even when the wind touches my shoulder,
I seldom hear voices. Only in dreams am I sure
to hear their voices.
The loveliest dream is a river that follows
its own sorely made path and seldom wavers.
As a friend said before his own death:
"My wife and I are living the dream."

•

When my lover speaks of death,
she never mentions God. In fact
she doesn't believe in any God I am familiar with.
In or out of dream, she has her reasons.
The heart within the heart of the coleus
is in part delicate
and entirely beautiful.

AUBADE, LAST MORNING IN ROME

When I kissed her,
I leaned over her.
Near the whelk-like whorl
of her deaf right ear,
I kissed her on the cheek
to awaken her.

THERE ARE MANY THINGS IN THE WORLD AND YOU

(a cento)

Yes, yours, my love, is the right human face.
What is this day with two suns in the sky?
And now I see with eye serene
The very pulse of the machine.
The breathing in unison
Of lovers whose bodies smell of each other.

Now slides the silent meteor on, and leaves
A shining furrow . . .
And will see you for the first time, perhaps
As God must see you.

Time was. Time is. Time shall be.
Had we but world enough, and time.
These pines, the fall oaks, these rocks
And thy lovely leaves among,
Awake for ever in a sweet unrest.
This love a moment known
For what I do not know.
It was never for the mean.
This is hard to say—
I am no good at love.

WINTER GHAZAL

Across the floor this rhombus of light.
Behind the sleeping boy specters that light

upon the wall. The shadow of a locust limb
lunging for the window. Outside . . . moonlight,

a lawn limned with frost, a glass globe salting
the street with its pearled light.

In the hallway a loose floorboard gives.
From beneath the doorsill a shim of light

the child stirs from a dead sleep to see.
To the south and east another strain of light.

At first the boy doesn't hear his father move
about the house or his father's light

humming or the hot and cold running water.
Awake he shuffles toward the light

coming from the bath, sees his father wash
in a raw and mostly silken light.

APPLE BLOSSOMS

More often than ever that spring,
my father filled bucket after ten gallon
bucket with immaculate white blossoms
raked from under the one stalwart apple tree,
from flower beds he carefully groomed.
Although he'd said as much before,
I knew when he insisted the apple tree
was dying, he said as much rather than say
he was dying. So whenever I saw him
carry another garbage pail filled with blossoms
to the alley, I took notice of the dirt
mixed with the stems, of the untold blossoms
he carried with him.

HOME GROWN TOMATOES

Not so long ago my father staked tomato plants
in uniform rows along the west wall of the garage.
Toward the end of summer he aligned the tomatoes
he'd picked like raw, succulent suns on twilled cotton
dish towels on the kitchen counter, then refused
to give me even one. Makes a kind of sense, though,
don't you think? They must have tasted *star-sweet*
to him, must have seemed as rare as the love of a woman.

ON THE ANNIVERSARY OF
MY FATHER'S BIRTH

Unlike other summer mornings
hoar frost whitens the grass.
Ghost-like behind a sea of fog,
the sun is more moon than sun.

Hoar frost whitens the grass.
As my father sets the thermostat,
(the sun more moon than sun)
he worries over the harvest.

As my father sets the thermostat,
coffee simmers on the stove.
He worries over the harvest,
mulls shipping the grain.

Coffee simmers on the stove.
My father washes and shaves,
mulls shipping the grain.
As I slip into the bathroom

my father washes and shaves.
With steam rising from the sink,
I slip into the bathroom.
He asks if I have gazed outside.

With steam rising from the sink,
he rinses soap from his face.
He asks if I have gazed outside.
He says, "Look east above the trees."

Unlike other summer mornings,
the dawn is like nothing I have seen.
Ghost-like behind a sea of fog,
the sun more moon than sun.

SO NEAR WAKING

My sleep is so near waking
I'm not sure my father
stepped into my room or I into his.
I'm not even sure he owns this house,
though I rifle through what I believe
is his chest of drawers, his desk.
A bit ill at ease, I leave
through the kitchen, step down
the three risers and out the back door
where I find myself as surprised as any
to see him entering then leaving
the garage, carrying an old rake and pail,
doing what he likes to call his *donkey work.*

When my father doesn't inhabit my dreams,
he's difficult to find. So why not keep him
here for a while? Surely there is no harm in this.
Of late, however, I've been thinking I should ask
for his forgiveness, though it would be easier
to ask how the weather is, if he's heard
from Mother. Having said as much,
I am certain of only this: that perhaps
I should leave him be, let him have his rest.

NO QUESTION

for my father

There's no question
he was as volatile as anyone.
Still when I walk, I walk with him.

In those last days we walked
short distances. He was unsteady.
There's no question, if he fell

I was there to help him to his feet.
We spoke of neighbors who'd passed
or moved on. Still I walk with him

even if others are near.
When alone I might speak to him.
There's no question I love him.

Until he died there wasn't a world
I knew without him, hidebound
or not. Still I walk with him

whether awake or dreaming
in the dark, moon or no moon.
I don't question it. Everywhere
I walk, I walk with him.

WINTER

Winter holds its ground.
The sky at its most luminous
a cobalt blue.
The ground rutted.
Ice thickening in the shade
of the corkscrew willow.

In the psychologist's office
I overhear someone
who resembles me say,
"I know women.
They leave or they die."
The sleeping dog stirs on the floor.
The melted and misshapen hands
on the clock in the Dali print
point toward that odd embrace
between time and waves
and what is a thin gruel of sky here.
In another frame a giraffe
on the Serengeti is set aflame
and takes off running.

Overnight the ice thickens.
A cold shiv of air cleaves
to the canyon walls, stirs my soul
when I walk everyday near campus.
For as long as I live I won't recall
the young woman leaving our house
to marry someone other than the baby's
father. I remember, though, a woman
who lay dying in a hospital room
overlooking the valley.

I've had a kind of sour taste
in my mouth as of late,
a fishy smell on my hands.
In the air around me the sour smell
of over-ripe suet. A small, cinched
bag of it left hanging from a nail
in the kitchen of every house
in which I have lived.

NOVEMBER 22, 1963

The air was as crisp and cool
as a new shirt folded and pinned
in cellophane. Across the playground
on the other side of the cyclone fence
in old man Roach's yard, small branches
and the few remaining leaves oscillate.
The sky a rinsed-out blue
above high cirrus clouds,
above the paper birch and silver maple,
above the oak where several lobed leaves
cling. George Coffey, pencil in hand,
stares through the mullioned window,
sketches trees on college rule paper.
The trees feel the weight of snow,
the dusting up of wind, the effects
of a recent freeze. Sister Gabriella
asks George to read from our
blue reader. She's pulling him in
from the trees, the border of sodden leaves
along the fence. He labors to pronounce
even the smallest words on the page.
In his hands they seem unsettled
in this room as do the trees in this wind.
Father Kelly appears in the hall,
knocks softly on the door.
He speaks briefly to Sister Gabriella.
Then returns again within the hour.
At his desk George draws a corkscrew
willow twisting in the wind.

DINNER AT CAFE CAMPAGNE

for Jeff Knorr, Albert Garcia, and Teresa Steinbach-Garcia

Over dinner I speak of a father
who was so angry
he did not speak from morning to dusk.
Even so when I left that evening,
I said, "I will see you in the morning."
Half way through my story, a fishing story,
Jeff is laughing. Then Albert
as our waitress glides by, refreshing
our drinks, seating a young father
and daughter near us.

Albert paints a portrait of his grandfather
who was forced as a boy to dig
his murdered father's grave,
then forced to unearth him
and bury him again.
The story doesn't end there
in the Mexican countryside
but in the States where he fled,
labored in lumber mills,
raised a family.

Jeff draws upon a recent outing
with his teenage son.
Early one morning, very little light,
no ducks in sight, he watches his son
fall asleep in their blind.
There's a tenderness to the details,
though a tincture of sadness, too.

The only time I hunted with my father,
he took off like a goat across the steep bluffs.
I wandered aimlessly for hours,
didn't see him again till late that afternoon.

Both men are laughing.
Caught up in it
I laugh till I am blind.

Albert's wife surveys the room.
She knows of fathers and sons.
Has had dinner with men like us
at tables like these.
I see her cast a glance
toward the young father and daughter,
then turn her gaze to us.
With the hint of a smile,
she offers what surely passes
as either prayer or admonition:
Breathe deep, boys.

BEFORE THERE WAS LIGHT

This evening, the moon, just this side of full,
is the same moon wherever men sleep.
Was there beautiful light at the end of your days
as Mother believed? Before there were any
references to eternal light in our home,
there was anger.

Mostly my father held a lid on his anger
during the day. Most days.
Mornings he went to work early like other fathers.
Feed dust fell or rested lightly there
on every surface and everywhere where there was light.
Though even under shadows there must have been
measurable movement and light.

With so little time left
why not speak in calmer tones?
There was a time when I was fearful
of the dark and could not sleep.
I was not much more than a baby.
An older brother, who no longer
speaks to me except in anger,
held my hand. When he told me this
not so long ago I remembered
the anger that flared like ground fire
in that house while Father was alive,
then flared again when he died.

SALVAGE

I don't believe in much these days,
though I believe everything my friend
told me the other evening. We talked
for an hour before I thought to ask
about her years in Missoula.
A graduate student and single mother,
she was raising a son, attending class,
working at the paper. She told me
she had a friend who would help her
with the baby, would babysit when needed,
would go with her to the laundromat
when she washed his diapers and bedding.
A bargain hunter, he scoured the county
for clothes, for books and vinyl records.
Would haunt salvage yards for bolts of cloth
and canned goods, the Northern Pacific spur
for loose grain and coal, grocery outlets
for remaindered goods and sundries.
Eventually he filled his house and garage
with what he found. After a time she
encouraged him to sort through it,
to go through each box. And so he did.
He was determined to catalogue all of it.
One day he brought clothes for the baby.
He'd found those in a box. On a crisp
October day, he brought his friend
a Burberry winter coat. It even fit.
"Like a glove," he liked to say,
"like a warm glove." For months
he worked at it, going through
every box in the house,
then started in on the garage.

He gave much of it, clothes and shoes,
to St. Vincent de Paul and to Goodwill.
To the Poverello Center he donated
other coats and shoes and cases
of canned meats and fish. Eventually,
he finished. One morning he dropped
by her house for coffee. He said, "You won't
believe this, but I wanted you to know
I finished this morning and in the last box,
in the very last box, wedged against the firewall
in the garage and painted on a rolled up canvas,
I found my own blue-eyed Jesus."

NOTES

Cento: A cento's original meaning derives from a term for a patched garment. In this case these centos (three in the text) are both patchwork and piecework of a kind. Two of these have multiple sources, taking one or two lines from a given work. The other, "How I Never Knew the Reason," (in homage to the late Richard Hugo) is comprised of lines taken exclusively from his third volume of poetry, *Good Luck in Cracked Italian.*

"Drifting Toward Sleep in Hedgerow, Normandy, 1944" is based in part on the WWII experiences of my uncle, Dick Collier.